AXIOMS FOR LIFE I

Mirelle Vraimont

AXIOMS FOR LIFE I

Copyright © 2006 by Lena Smith Carter as a compilation of axioms.

The "sayings" in this work are an original collection of axioms submitted to the manufacturer by the named individual author/publisher. The author/publisher confirms the authenticity and originality of the axioms and the manufacturer is neither liable nor obligated to authenticate the same.

The views expressed in this book do not reflect the views of the manufacturer or members of the manufacturing staff. These views are solely inured to the author/publisher.

Under the copyright laws of the United States of America, this book is protected, with all the rights and privileges appertaining thereto. This book may not be reproduced, shared, electronically reproduced nor copied by any other means not approved by written consent of the author.

Manufactured in the United States of America by:

www.lulu.com

ISBN: 978-0-6151-3698-1

DEDICATION

To my mother:

M. A. Briggs, an elegant and knowledgeable Southern lady!

For all my endeavors, you have offered encouragement, guidance, and love. You brought the wisdom of Grandma Amanda, which she so aptly instilled in you during her short time on this earth. I thank you for all that you brought and for sharing, caring, giving and most of all, for loving me!

                                                          m.v.

FOREWORD

What is said to you as you journey through life will stay with you forever. If it is good, it will influence your life for the better. If it is negative, it will provide a constant source of sadness.

We thrive on things that lift us up and inspire us! Just think of the radiant smiles of a child when he is paid a compliment; if you are given a promotion at your job for good work, how elated you are!

Remember always that words are like swords. If sheathed and properly used, they are wonderful protection. If unsheathed and
improperly used, they can do considerable harm.

These axioms have come your way at different times, "clothed in different clothing." The upcoming volumes will explore more "saws" from this country and around the world!
Let me hear from you!

                        Mirelle Vraimont
                www.dseyafanel@hotmail.com

Every sunrise is a new opportunity to succeed.

**What one constantly thinks
will become a reality.**

**In the winter of your life,
think spring!**

**How are words like knives?
Once they cut you,
the scar remains!**

If you are smart, don't tell anyone!

**If you are always prepared,
when the fire springs forth,
you'll have water.**

**Don't make a promise
you can't keep!**

Write love letters only if you don't care if they are published.

A couple's first day is the basis of the rest of their children's lives.

Children are born with a *tabula rasa* (clean slate). Be careful what you place upon it!

**Love tinges everything
it touches.**

Constructive criticism is a valuable tool; criticism for the sake of criticism is cruel!

Secrets are a bond when kept; a catastrophe when revealed!

**A woman cannot change a man;
she can only change herself!**

Lowered eyes signify an embattled spirit!

A song can lift the heaviest of burdens.

Grief shared is grief relieved.

**Faithfulness is the halo of
a successful marriage.**

To parade ignorant people as intellectuals is the ultimate insult.

Music transforms the disfigured soul!

**Lovers are to each other
as the sun is to the moon.**

There will always be occasions where silence is mandatory.

Exceptional people usually have exceptional parents!

Good manners are the result of constant practice.

A hug can alleviate a weary soul!

An insincere compliment is worse than no compliment at all.

The mask of hypocrisy is often transparent.

**What the lips do not tell,
the eyes surely will!**

**Transient perfection should
be admired.**

Evil thoughts are transported at lightning speed.

**Equality opens the door;
injustice slams it shut!**

**Persistence is an enigma of
the enslaved.**

Do not ignore illiteracy. It can inhibit the power to think!

Fear paralyzes!

**The creative mind shows you
what you cannot see!**

Health is priceless!

**A poem can paint a picture
in the dark!**

Compliance is a necessary implement of subordination.

Inconsistency spawns indecision.

If happiness knocks, open the door!

The warmth of a smile symbolizes the luminescence of the heart.

**Twinkling stars remind us of
our diminution in the
universe.**

**Grains of sand on a beach,
though temporarily repressed,
are refreshed with the tide!**

If you find yourself in a crisis, be decisive!

When a task requires exertion, think only of the strength you'll build; not the attendant fatigue.

Moderation is the balancer for both extravagance and miserliness! Experiment with life; you never know what the outcome will be.

**Have something in common
with exotic flowers:
Always smell great!**

An expert has an edge; he knows his "files."

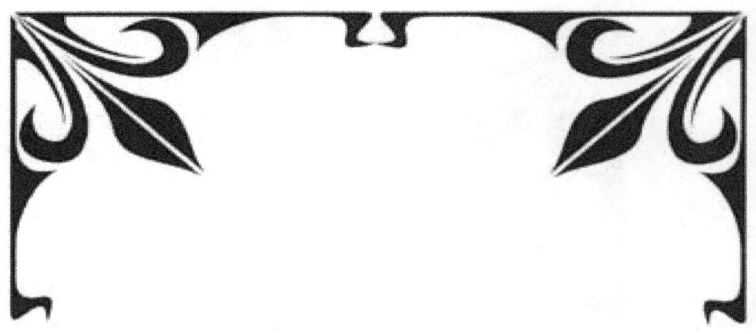

A flag will send chills up your spine even as it burns!

If others walk on you, demonstrate your resilience!

There is something to be said for the military: Obedience knows its rank.

**Obesity is rampant because
food is plenteous!**

Unless you examine the facts carefully, you will not be able to dispute the outcome!

Trust, once broken, is irreparable!

To obliterate hate, choose every opportunity to teach love!

An ersatz alto is often an erstwhile soprano.

A good education allows one to avoid a servile lifestyle.

Knowing the direction you are going allows you to avoid misplacing your energies.

The likelihood of failure is ever present: Defeat it with achievement!

Repetition is a great learning tool. If you don't believe it, check the octaves of a piano: All the same.

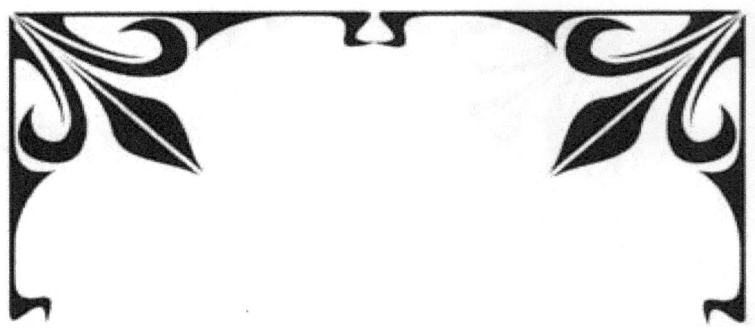

**A suitcase is like a dishwasher;
it holds the things you need
to wash.**

**If you regard your peers with
scorn, in your absence,
they'll regard you
with laughter.**

A scandal is usually a disclosure of juicy facts.

If you are dissatisfied with everything, you will dissatisfy everyone.

What fits a king is not always fit for a king.

**Romantic words are beautiful
but can also be deceitful.**

Identify your friends before your enemies arrive!

A woman can be effective and beautiful: Helen of Troy's beauty is as legendary as the Trojan horse's effectiveness.

Apathy is not an exemplary quality!

How is a bunch of flowers like a bunch of grapes? Refreshing, fragrant, and colorful!

Corruption precedes ultimate decline!

Every sunset should remind you that you were spared another day!

A rose is the headdress of a thorn!

Ignorance of etiquette can stymie an otherwise perfect encounter.

**If you can't converse without
a drink, don't converse!**

**During the birth experience,
the excruciating pain of
incoming life is exacerbated
by outgoing life!**

A full moon reminds us that illumination can come from many sources.

The harbor is a perfect shelter for disabled vessels; where should disabled thinkers go?

If you are a perfectionist who desires pinpoint exactitude, get a pin cushion.

Pain is the flip side of comfort!

**Avoid tablecloths with wrinkles;
They need pressing and
don't impress!**

If you don't think salmon are tenacious, try swimming upstream!

A sign of sadness: A smile that does not reach the eyes!

Belief is a powerful tool!

Change is the equivalent of development!

**Prejudice is the incubation
and nurturance of
outmoded ideas!**

Poverty withers the soul!

The worth of a human being is not measured by his color!

A look can shrivel a soul as easily as a dagger kills!

A breeze is God's kiss!

Take every opportunity to avoid extinguishing the light in the eyes of a child. That light equals intellect!

If there were no buds, there would be no flowers!

Existing on this earth is an exercise in interdependence.

Personality is a natural endowment.

Mirelle Vraimont is an internationally renowned concert artist who has traveled to more than fifteen different countries in the pursuit of excellence in her craft and whose life experiences have bordered on everything from the tragic to the hilarious; from shocking misfortune to extreme good fortune; from anguish to contentment.

In addition to her international concert tours, she is a published author, poet, and philosopher; teacher, parent, publisher, and patent holder.

Each individual's life experiences, while different and personal, are often mirrored in the life experiences of others. Our mothers, grandmothers, grandfathers, aunts, uncles, great-aunts, teachers, etc., all gave us statements to provide a series of life's lessons according to their experiences.

Mirelle wrote this book with the hope that you will see yourself and some of those around you in these pages and that these reminders will continue to provide life's lessons.

www.ingramcontent.com/pod-product-compliance
Lightning Source LLC
Chambersburg PA
CBHW031000090426
42737CB00007B/615